PRAISE FOR *You Don't Miss Your Water*

"Cornelius Eady's new book is alive with passionate irony, with joy of language, and with unsentimental grief. I love the way it moves from the recent to the less-recent past, and then back again—forth and back across the sill of death, following the deep heart's chronology, the Kronology past blame, struck with the sorrow and energy and humor of reality, the inherited pain and wonder of family, race, history, and gender. *You Don't Miss Your Water* is the work not of an optimist or a pessimist, but a realist. Eady does not limit his vision to what he might wish to see, and sees instead what is there: human stubbornness, longing, dreaming, rage, transcendence, intransigence. He has made a fierce document of great intimacy and scope. This is a well we will come to over and over, to drink of its knowledge and music."

—SHARON OLDS

"Who wants wisdom will find it here, but will be able to *breathe* under its introduction. Obviously the poet is committed to positives. He of the *involved* voice is determined; direct; alert; confident."

—GWENDOLYN BROOKS

"*You Don't Miss Your Water* is a gem. Twenty-one poems for any man to put in his pocket whenever he leave his father's house. These poems are blue psalms about life, family, and death. Cornelius Eady opens his heart and gives us poetry filled with tears and strength. There is so much honesty in this book it forces the reader to look into the mirror before the *well runs dry.*"

—E. ETHELBERT MILLER

YOU DON'T MISS YOUR WATER

BY CORNELIUS EADY

Kartunes
Victims of the Latest Dance Craze
Boom, Boom, Boom: A Chapbook
The Gathering of My Name
You Don't Miss Your Water
The Autobiography of a Jukebox
Brutal Imagination

YOU DON'T MISS YOUR WATER

POEMS BY

Cornelius Eady

CARNEGIE MELLON UNIVERSITY PRESS
PITTSBURGH 2004

Library of Congress Control Number: 2003112549
ISBN 0-88748-416-6
Printed and bound in the United States of America
First Carnegie Mellon University Press Edition, 2004

10 9 8 7 6 5 4 3 2 1

You Don't Miss Your Water was first published by
Henry Holt and Company, Inc., in 1995.

The publisher would like to express his gratitude to James
Reiss and James W. Hall for their assistance in producing
this volume.

Some of the poems in this collection have appeared, at times in different forms, in the following periodicals:

Agni: "Paradiso"; *Colorado Review*: "I Ain't Got No Home"; *Drumvoices Review*: "Papa Was a Rolling Stone"; *Global City Review*: "The Chapel of Love," "Going Down Slow," "Money"; *Pequod*: "I Know (I'm Losing You)," "A Little Bit of Soap," "One Kind Favor," "Fetchin' Bones," "Soothe Me," "A Rag, a Bone, and a Hank of Hair," "I Just Wanna Testify," "You Don't Miss Your Water"; *Phoebe*: "Motherless Children"; *Seneca Review*: "All God's Dangers"; *Red Brick Review*: "It's Only a Paper Moon."

This book is for Alveta Hayes.

ACKNOWLEDGMENTS

I would like to thank the John Simon Guggenheim
Memorial Foundation, The Writer's Room, Inc., the
Squaw Valley Community of Writers, and the Millay
Colony for the Arts for providing me the time and
space to work on this book.

I would also like to thank the Rockefeller Foundation
for its generous fellowship to its Study and
Conference Center in Bellagio, Italy.

Finally, deep gratitude to the many friends and
colleagues whose advice and encouragement kept
me at it—in particular, Toi Derricotte, Shreela Ray,
Sharon Olds, Galway Kinnell, Jason Shinder, Liz
Rosenburg, Mary Oliver, Molly Malone Cook, and
Julie Bruck.

CONTENTS

And it's damage that we do
and never know,
It's the words that we don't say
that scare me so.

—ELVIS COSTELLO
"Accidents Will Happen"

But when you left me,
O, how I cried.
You don't miss your water
'til your well runs dry.

—WILLIAM BELL
"You Don't Miss Your Water"

YOU DON'T MISS YOUR WATER

I KNOW (I'M LOSING YOU)

Have you ever touched your father's back? No,
my fingers tell me, as they try to pull up a similar
memory.

There are none. This is a place we have never
traveled to, as I try to lift his weary body onto the
bedpan.

I recall a photo of him standing in front of our
house. He is large, healthy, a stocky body in a dark
blue suit.

And now his bowels panic, feed his mind phony
information, and as I try to position him, my hands
shift, and the news shocks me more than the sight
of his balls.

O, bag of bones, this is all I'll know of his body,
the sharp ridge of spine, the bedsores, the ribs rising
up in place like new islands.

I feel him strain as he pushes, for nothing, feel his
fingers grip my shoulders. *He is slipping to dust,* my
hands inform me, *you'd better remember this.*

One of the things my father never liked about me was my dark skin. *You used to be so pretty* was the way he'd put it, and it was true, there is proof, a baby picture of a curly-haired, just a hair's breadth away from fair skinned child, me, my small fingers balled up into fists.

And then, as if some God shrugged and suddenly turned away its gaze, something caved in, and I was dark, dark, and all that it implied.

So what happened? My father always seemed to want me to explain, what did this desertion mean? This skin that seemed born to give up, this hair that crinkled to knots, this fairy tale–like transformation?

You used to look real good, my father, a man of slightly lighter hue, would say to me, his son, his changeling. *Maybe you ought to wash more.*

ONE KIND FAVOR

My father is close to death, and in his final hours, he begins his journey by asking anyone within earshot of his bed for a few things.

He asks to be allowed to go back home to Florida.

He asks to be able to cast off his dreary hospital gown, to be reunited to the shape of his own clothes.

He wants someone to fetch him his shoes, now useless for weeks, the impossible act of slipping them on, the slight miracle of bending and tying.

In his wishes, my mother arrives and sits at his bedside, or he changes it, and he walks back into his house, into the living room, his old chair.

He is so close to dreaming now, and his body lifts with the desire to fix things.

My father's a sealed tin of dust, riding in the trunk of my rental car.

My sister and niece are in the back seat, and I choose not to inform them of this.

Later, I will meet with my cousin at the church where the memorial service was held.

I will set the box on the curb while we talk.

I am carting around the rubble of the man who loved to call me stupid, who made my sister feel like nothing, who drove my mother nuts.

I have done this in order to shave a few dollars off the funeral costs, I tell myself, as a small part of me gives in, fans the smoldering pleasure.

SOOTHE ME

What happened to my money? My father asks me this
toward the end of one of my visits to the hospital,
and I think he must mean the large wad of cash he
loves to flash and carry, the only leverage he thinks
an old man has over the world, the thing I love the
least about him, skinflint, miser, money-grubber,
tight-fisted ruler of the house.

But no, it's smaller; he's talking petty cash.

Look over there in that drawer, he says, *don't you
see it?*

I see just what I expect: tongue depressors, baby
oil, the diabetic candy he sniffed and left by the side
of the road. If there was any cash there, it is long
gone, a secret boon for some nurse or orderly, a
justifiable tax for a hard-ass patient.

So why don't I tell him the truth? Instead, I reach
in my wallet, ask him, *you mean this?* And he watches
me as I do, and believes it; he robs me of twenty
bucks, and I let him.

I remember the strength left in his fingers, the way they clamped around the bill. If it was a kiss, we'd tease, *who's your girlfriend?* If it was a moment in a song, the lyric would sing, *without you, I'm nothing.*

A RAG, A BONE, AND A HANK OF HAIR

I'm sitting alone with my father at the funeral parlor. Viewing hours have just begun, but it's midday work week, and for a few hours it'll be just me and him, the first time I've laid eyes on him since the phone call woke me up.

I'm doing what a son is supposed to do, or so I've been told, but it's hard work, sitting with what used to love and trouble you.

Of course, his body is a bright lie in its casket, everything that has brought him here carefully hidden or rearranged.

Is there something I want to tell him? Anything I can forgive?

I can only sit and wait and listen to the gospel music as it buzzes though the speakers. *Jesus, Jesus, Jesus.* All his time, all his struggles that I still call life. All his trials.

The house has gone down, I try to tell my father in the
hospital, *it isn't worth that much anymore.*

He won't have any of it, this man who has kept
such a shining memory of what he's bought with his
hands so close to his heart, so close to what he knows
he's made of, that I'm reduced to a bogeyman who
happens to wear his son's face.

I tell him he's been overpaying his taxes on it for
years, this stingy man who has been forced to go
through so many quick changes these last few
months.

Mr. Bones is prying my father's hands, finger by
finger, away from the things that he knows of this
world, and this latest revelation's a major blow,
something I can tell is twisting his life into
meaningless shapes.

Far better to think his silly boy, the one who earns
his living from talking funny, has once again
misunderstood the way this world's supposed to
work.

Uh-uh! he shoots back, eyes expanding to take in all God's dangers. This is how life, sharpened to a fine point, plunges into what we call hope. This is how death, if it's given enough time, irons out the small details.

How many ways do I want to kill this woman, this
young bureaucrat at the Office of Social Services, for
wanting to kill me? Kill me slowly by degrees, kill me
with provisions, kill me in measured words, kill my
mother by rubbing her sad life with my father in her
face. O, how this woman, bored, dulled by repetition,
wants my mother officially rendered inert, reduced
to a mere boarder in a broken-down ghetto house,
how she wants the word *bastard* to define our
conversation.

What did I say or do? Who knows, but I do know
this look she's giving me, after telling me that there's
no place for my mother's well-being in their
guidelines, that as far as they're concerned, she isn't
even legally a part of my family. I know this look.
This woman wants to observe a screamer, a ripper,
she wants her dreams of a babbling monkey to rise.

Blow up, she whispers, as she explains what she
isn't going to do for me, how my father's bound to
disappear, item by item, first his house, then his cars,

then all his money except for what it takes for a pine box and a hole.

She thinks she's the facts of life, a wall with no apparent handholds, the river referred to in the old spirituals: deep, wide, fraught with many sorrows, and her eyes dare me to become a nigger and kick over the table.

A few weeks before my father dies, my sister tells me
a fuzzy story about a young woman she'd heard
rumors about, a class or two ahead of her in high
school, who carried our unusual last name.

And when my niece goes through some of my
father's papers, she uncovers a small, laminated card,
a birth certificate from a midwestern state, for a boy,
born a year before I was, though it's a different last
name.

What about this? We want to know, and we
badger my father in the hospital, until he finally
admits to us that the woman my sister tried but
never got to meet in high school was indeed our
half-sister.

My father tells us that when my niece was an
infant, and my sister was living away in Florida, he'd
bundle my niece up and take her to this woman's
apartment. He was that proud of being a grandfather,
and he knew my niece would be too young to
remember.

She married a rich man, and they moved away to Israel is as far as he's willing to take us on this. *She's happy, and I don't want to bother her.*

And the birth certificate? I see language in the way the bones in his thin body twist; his mouth says, *beats me.*

He's pissed off that it's come down to this, that his children would have enough time to try and unravel a man's business.

And then he clucked, which I took to mean *what makes you think I owe you this?*

She's a poor, wandering soul, this woman I recognize
at my hometown library. She's come in to escape the
brief rain, this woman whom we have always known
in town as a person of no fixed address, a person who
attended poetry readings or political meetings only
for the eats at the reception (thus being one of the
most honest people in town), the same calm, almost
beneficent features, the same long, stringy hair, if a
bit grayer, body still moving as though she'd be able
to float, if the thought would ever cross her mind.
In another culture, she might have been considered
holy, if not for the way her eyes flash if you happen
to wander too close, if not for her sailor's tongue,
which will always slap away your dreamy first
impressions of her.

She's still alive, I tell my sister-in-law, who
remembers when she happens to call that evening.

We trade all the stories we hold about this woman,
who, had she a house to live in, would be known as
the neighborhood "witch," the person the children

on the block would feel honor-bound to tease and
fear, and think of if they ever had need to define the
word *strange*.

Before seeing her, I had spent most of the day
trying to keep my mother distracted. We had to call
in a plumber in order to repair the shoddy, back-alley
work my father and cousin had done on the
bathroom fixtures, a series of cheap, head-scratching,
seat-of-the-pants decisions that resulted in my mother
being forced to lug buckets of hot water from the
kitchen (*Jack and Jillin'*, she calls it) in order to take
her nightly bath.

Some part of her struggles to keep this fact at the
front of her mind as the plumber roams the house,
pokes about as if adopted without consent. We are
trying to keep her diverted because, as far as my
mother's concerned, this constitutes an invasion.
We have tried to tell her she has nothing to worry
about, but she knows she doesn't own the house,
and she's lived her life with a sweet-talker.

She worries that this is yet another fast one, that
she might be witnessing the beginning of a process
that will land her either in a mental hospital or in the
street. She's nervous, and she lets me in on her state

of mind the way she always does, by speaking in long,
sometimes biblical allegories.

She wants me to know *the bible foretold
Watergate,* which really means, *don't you do nothing
behind my back.* She speaks of the dangers of secrets,
of things she had to learn about her unwed husband
by shock, by accident.

And she tells me a story about a homeless woman,
not the person I saw at the library, clothed with
nothing but the rags on her back, and with the few
possessions a cart could carry, wandering our block,
looking for a handout.

And there wasn't a single charitable soul on our
entire street that day, not even my mother, at first,
who turns the woman down, then watches as she
travels from door to door, only to be told by the
neighbors, *hand full of gimme, mouth full of much
obliged,* who watches as the woman wanders back,
low-down and empty-handed.

So I give her two dollars, my mother says, a spy
banging away at the pipes upstairs, small prayers in
her eyes.

Did Daddy ever take you out dancing? I ask my
mother as we sit watching the soaps in the living
room. I'd heard a story from one of my aunts about
my parents' early days together, something about a
double date my aunt went along on to a dance hall.

My mother either doesn't remember it too well
or has decided against letting me in too closely on
this one. *No, it wasn't me,* she grumps. *It must have
been some other woman.*

He would take her to the movies, though. Once
she even browbeat him into taking her to see the
Mills Brothers.

And I'd forgotten what a big deal they once were.
She tells me it was an event that was talked about
weeks before the concert at the hotel where she was
working as a maid.

It was an event large enough to test the mettle of a
young couple. When her friends at work asked, *Are
you going, Alveta?* it was clearly a question about
her man.

And it felt good to hear that at least once, my father did her right.

Did they laugh easy there? Did they clap and toss off their low-waged week?

Did the brothers sing my mother's favorite song, "Paper Moon"?

Her favorite song. It's a question I'd never thought to ask until this moment, and now as she answers I notice her eyes as they swing back, and I hear her recite a hidden line or two until suspicion slams the door.

THE WAY YOU DO THE THINGS YOU DO

Okay: my daddy wasn't what you'd call a model parent. He was stingy, and his life sometimes gave his jokes a nasty edge that didn't fit the punch line, like the time he and a Puerto Rican neighbor gave me a cup of dark liquid, named it Kool-Aid just to watch an innocent tongue spit wine.

This afternoon, as my father lies unhealed in the hospital, my sister pulls up the story of the winter she had to shame him into buying me a coat by going downtown to Woolworth's and lifting one off the rack. It had become clear to her that he wasn't about to do anything, and she got sick of watching my back slump in the wind.

Now she adds a piece of the story she's carried for years: how can she tell her brother how a father decides that a child isn't a part of his property? We both know he's wrong, my mother backs us up, and he'll claim the same later with my retarded brother, but it sets a soul to wandering.

Months after my father's death, I have a dream. My wife and I check into what should be a "good" hotel, except nobody's bothered to straighten up our room. The sheets are soiled and jumbled, the kitchen alive with debris.

As I call the desk to complain, I feel my stomach sink the way it does before one's about to talk to a mechanic. *Why,* I think to myself, *do they think I have this coming? What did I do to deserve this?* What did they read on my face that told them *he won't squawk?*

And now, alas, it is too late. My wife and I are trying
to tell my mother how wise it would be for her to
finally marry my father, now that he is lying, half a
shade, in the hospital.

His doctors feel he'll be dying slow, and he's
burning up his pensions. Soon he will have to go on
Medicaid, and the rules are firm. Single men that
have made no provisions must sign practically
everything over to the Government, must, in their
ironic terms, "spend down" to an income they
haven't seen since they were starting out, must
whittle their desires to small items, chewing gum,
haircuts, playing cards; must transform themselves,
whether they want it or not, from homeowners to
paupers.

Though they've lived together for over forty years,
as far as the Government's concerned, without a
paper, my mother is simply the woman he's been
keeping. If they're not married, and soon, she'll lose
the house.

My father tells us he's willing, but when we bring
this up with my mother, she answers with the voice
I know she had on the day that she finally saw how
things were with my father, that they would never
wed; the young woman who decided with her last
drop of self-worth that a part of his one good thing
had come and gone.

What a cold day that must have been in her heart.
She will never visit him in the hospital. And now, in
a voice that could damn a saint, she is telling us
she'd rather starve on her anger than feed off his
slow regret.

My daddy is refusing to eat. He has been in the
hospital too long; he has had to watch as one of his
many roommates, a quiet black gentleman about his
age, passes away in the night; he has to lie alone in a
bed and watch his own torso dwindle away, to be
patient as his pants and shoes become obsolete.

As soon as he eats, he has to go to the bathroom,
and the man can no longer walk, cannot rise an adult
from his bed; cannot shut the bathroom door behind
him, the word *private,* impossible magic, never to be
his again.

The man my daddy has become cannot deal with
more than a thimble of food, and he will not get
adjusted to a world of harassed nurses and public
bedpans. He will let most of his meals lay fallow on
their trays.

He will glare at his son's persistence with the
anger the sick have for what a healthy body can't
know. He will force you to smell the blossoming of
his terrible resolve. He would rather die.

And at last, I get the phone call. The blues rolls into my sleepy ears at five A.M., a dry, official voice from my father's hospital. A question, a few quick facts, and my daddy's lying upstate on the coolin' floor.

Death, it seems, was kinder to him in his last hour than life was in his last four months.

Death, who pulls him to a low ebb, then slowly floods over his wrecked body like a lover.

Cardio-vascular collapse, the polite voice is telling me, but later my cousin tells me he arrives on the ward before they shut my father's eyes and mouth to see the joy still resting on his face from the moment my daddy finally split his misery open.

MONEY (THAT'S WHAT I WANT)

My father has just died, and now I must stand in line
at the Manhattan branch of his bank in order to
withdraw funds from his accounts before they find
out and freeze them in probate.

My daddy is gone, but if I want to give him a
proper burial, I must begin this last dance with him.
I must stuff my pockets with his mojo, the greenback
dollar, the one true spell he ever believed in, and then
walk two awkward blocks from his bank to mine.

The teller takes his time checking me out. He can
smell that something isn't quite right, but since my
power of attorney is in working order, we both know
how this transaction must end.

He must count my father's leavings into my hand.
How transparent my pockets will feel under the
midday New York sun. How nervous my steps as
I carry him.

ANOTHER MAN DONE GONE

It is nearly time for my father's memorial service;
today the blues comes calling on my mother, who
still harbors doubts about his passing.

The blues will dress us up to get her attention.
Your man done gone, says my new dark suit. He is
gone, not in the ways she knows; not until her old
fool husband comes home; it is a leaving that will
begin to turn the things she knows of him, his chair,
his old cars, his shabby clothes behind the door,
into husks.

My mother sees that there are too many relatives
in the house for this to be some kind of put-on. The
blues slowly begins to readjust her eyes, and here is
what I notice: she does not laugh, she will not cry,
she cannot follow as we exit to let him go.

There was, at the end, a look of great peace on my
father's face at the moment of his death. At the
memorial service my cousin tells this story to us as
a way to infer a last-minute salvation, a meeting of
Jesus in the middle of the air, this being, after all, the
AME Zionist church across from the vacant lot that
used to be the elementary school me and my sister
attended.

This is the part of the service where we stand up
for him, this small knot of family and friends in a very
large room.

He's gone and left my mother with nothing. Her
name isn't on the deed to the house, her name never
appears on his policies. Her mind's confused, she
can't take care of herself by herself, and I'm having
a real hard time convincing various agencies that she
even exists.

Which is why there is no casket to bear. Too
expensive, we decide, money to be better spent on
the living, on my mother.

Still, we give him a family send-off. *A hard man, but his own man!* sing the testimonies. *A stingy man, but a family man!* And I truthfully thank him for the roof he put over our heads, for staying when a lot of other men took a look at their wives, their babies, their house bills and changed their names to fare-thee-well.

And then my sister stands up, stands up through the pain and accidents of first born, first torn, stands up, the family's "bad girl," the willful daughter, low-down spirit of red dresses and iodine, my sister stands up in a way I can't fully explain, but know belongs to black women, she stands up and declares, *I'm just like him, but I'm a woman, so I can't get away with it.*

At home, my mother wakes up and spends some of
her day talking back to my father's empty chair.

In Florida, my sister experiences the occasional
dream in which my father returns; they chat.

He's been dead and gone for a little over a year.
How it would please me to hear his unrecorded voice
again, now alive only in the minds of those who
remember him.

If I could, if as in the old spiritual, I could actually
get a direct phone link to the other side, I could call
him up, tell him about this small prize of a week I've
had teaching poetry at a ski resort a few miles from
Lake Tahoe, imagination jackpot, brief paradise of
letters.

How could I make him believe that I have gotten
all of this, this modern apartment, this pond in front
of my window, all from the writing of a few good
lines of verse, my father, who distrusted anything he
couldn't get his hands on?

Most likely, he would listen, then ask me, as he
always did, just for safety's sake, if my wife still had
her good-paying job.

And I can't tell you why, but this afternoon,
I wouldn't become hot and stuffy from his concern,
think "old fool," and gripe back *of course I'm still
teaching college. It's summer, you know?*

This afternoon, I miss his difficult waters. And
when he'd ask, as he always would, *how're they
treating you?* I'd love to answer back, *Fine, Daddy.
They're paying me to write about your life.*

DEUCE AND A QUARTER

(for Tom Ellis)

The dust of my father the furnace missed
Is here in his Buick Electra 225
That has been parked, unopened,
In the driveway since his death.
In order to sell it,
We exhume the door to look for papers,

And (surprise) here is his sweat,
Mingled with pitted chrome and wasps' nests.
Bridle with no horse, plow without a field,
Not even the house was his like this.

And now his death
Is everyday business,
And I am any son
Who must finally remove the plates,
Then phone a truck to pull
This collision away;
A car, like any car.

In Italy, a scholar is giving an after-dinner talk on
her study of Dante and the many questions left
unanswered about the afterlife.

For example, where does the shade of the body,
the one true and indestructible rainbow vessel, go to
wait for the end of time if the head goes one way at
the moment of death, and the limbs another?

And I thought of my father, fired to dust in a plain
urn, and all the answers I'd learned in church, how
all the lost must rise, commuters home at last, from
wherever fate has ditched them, with their
dishonored ropes and blown equipment, up from the
sea, the peat, the misjudged step, the angry fuselage,
the air bright from ashes, as will and memory knit.

Will my father's glorified body be the one I'd
grown up with, a stocky man, perhaps dressed in his
one good suit?

Will he be the young boy I'll never know, Sonny
Eady, who wanders off for months at a time, always
returning with no accounting of his movements?

Will he be the groom my mother saw, or the shape
of the man she claims visited her weeks after his
funeral, appearing just to help my mother close this
file on their lives, just to tell her *fare-thee-well,*
woman, I'll never see you no more?

How can this be done? is one question the scholar
is here to work on, and as she places our hands into
Dante's, and night gathers in the mountains, I think
that every hymn is a flare of longing, that the key to
any heaven is language.

The Gathering of My Name

"Eady, who won the Lamont Prize for his 1985 collection, deserves further recognition for the wisdom and virtuosity of his latest."

—*Ploughshares*

"Unstaged, unadorned, the poems are true characterizations, tributes to Muddy Waters, John Coltrane, Thelonious Monk."

—*The Village Voice*

"Through the clarity of his perceptions and the earnest, playful music of his language, Eady finds transcendent moments in everyday experience."

—*The Plum Review*

"Most impressive about this collection is Eady's ability to use language to translate, through evocation, what can't be translated directly without tremendous loss of resonance. He does this brilliantly enough in his poems that evoke dynamics of music, but he does it at an even more effective level in several poems that translate the experience of being Black in America. It's no easy thing, at this time, for an African-American poet to find language that breaks through sociological and political configurations to sting us directly and afresh with a taste of his or her experience."

—*The Kenyon Review*

Victims of the Latest Dance Craze

"Following the laughter and the compassionate pith of a dauntless imagination, these poems beeline or zig-zag always to the jugular, the dramatic and unarguable revelation of the heart."

—JUNE JORDAN

"What a dancer he is! His hoofing with language more than holds its own with the ritualized dancing evoked in his poetry."

—*The Village Voice*

"There's a knife-edge clarity under the voice, intricate rhythm patterns threaded through the lines, an improvisational feeling that doesn't pull against the poetry. There isn't any linguistic sleight of hand happening in his poetry; the emotion and motion feel grounded to the earth."

—YUSEF KOMUNYAKAA

"His poems have the shaggy wildness of Frank O'Hara's. Like O'Hara, Mr. Eady is a poet who loves an audience.... There is much to admire in Mr. Eady's work—his inventiveness, his eye for detail, his interest in the lives of others."

—*The New York Times Book Review*